anythink

How do animals change?

Bobbie Kalman

 Crabtree Publishing Company
www.crabtreebooks.com

Created by Bobbie Kalman

Author and Editor-in-Chief
Bobbie Kalman

Educational consultants
Elaine Hurst
Joan King
Jennifer King

Notes for adults
Jennifer King

Editors
Kathy Middleton
Crystal Sikkens

Design
Bobbie Kalman
Katherine Berti

Photo research
Bobbie Kalman

Print and production coordinator
Katherine Berti

Prepress technician
Katherine Berti

Illustrations
Barbara Bedell: pages 11, 23
Bonna Rouse: pages 5, 7 (eggs)
Margaret Amy Salter: pages 7 (background), 19
Tiffany Wybouw: page 3

Photographs
BigStockPhoto: page 9
iStockPhoto: page 5 (top right)
Other photographs by Shutterstock

Library and Archives Canada Cataloguing in Publication

Kalman, Bobbie, 1947-
    How do animals change? / Bobbie Kalman.

(My world)
Includes index.
Issued also in electronic format.
ISBN 978-0-7787-9568-1 (bound).--ISBN 978-0-7787-9593-3 (pbk.)

    1. Animal life cycles--Juvenile literature. 2. Growth--Juvenile
literature. I. Title. II. Series: My world (St. Catharines, Ont.)

QL49.K333 2011   j591.56   C2010-907450-5

Library of Congress Cataloging-in-Publication Data

Kalman, Bobbie.
  How do animals change? / Bobbie Kalman.
      p. cm. -- (My world)
  Includes index.
  ISBN 978-0-7787-9593-3 (pbk. : alk. paper) -- ISBN 978-0-7787-9568-1
(reinforced library binding : alk. paper) -- ISBN 978-1-4271-9675-0
(electronic (pdf))
  1. Animal life cycles--Juvenile literature. I. Title.
QL49.K2943 2011
591.3'9--dc22

                                    2010047127

Crabtree Publishing Company

www.crabtreebooks.com   1-800-387-7650

Printed in China/022011/RG20101116

Published in Canada
Crabtree Publishing
616 Welland Ave.
St. Catharines, Ontario
L2M 5V6

Published in the United States
Crabtree Publishing
PMB 59051
350 Fifth Avenue, 59th Floor
New York, New York 10118

Published in the United Kingdom
Crabtree Publishing
Maritime House
Basin Road North, Hove
BN41 1WR

Published in Australia
Crabtree Publishing
386 Mt. Alexander Rd.
Ascot Vale (Melbourne)
VIC 3032

What is in this book?

Hatching from eggs   4

Mother turtle leaves   6

Mammals are born   8

Mothers and babies   10

Learning as they grow   12

Looking alike   14

Changing their coats   16

Butterfly changes   18

Changes in newts   20

Dragonfly changes   22

Words to know and Index   23

Hatching from eggs

Animals start their lives in different ways.

Some animals **hatch** from eggs.

To hatch is to break out of an egg.

These baby crocodiles are hatching.

Which other animals hatch from eggs?

Turtles hatch
from eggs.

Snakes hatch
from eggs.

Birds hatch
from eggs.

Mother turtle leaves

Many baby animals that hatch from eggs look after themselves. A sea turtle mother lays eggs on the beach and then goes back to the ocean.

1. Mother turtle lays eggs.

2. The sea turtle mother goes back to the ocean after she has laid her eggs.

Baby sea turtles look after themselves after they hatch.

3. The baby turtles hatch.

4. They dig themselves out of the sand.

5. They walk to the ocean and swim away.

Mammals are born

Some animals do not hatch from eggs.

They are **born**, just like you.

Mammals are animals that are born.

This baby lamb was just born.

It is a mammal.

Mammal mothers feed their babies milk.
The milk is made in their bodies.
These fox **kits**, or babies, are **nursing**.
Nursing is drinking mother's milk.
As the kits grow, they will start
eating other foods, too.

Mothers and babies

Many mammal mothers care for
their babies for a long time.
The babies grow, change, and learn.
Then they become fully grown **adults**.
These changes are part of a **life cycle**.

A life cycle starts with a new baby.
It ends when the baby grows into
an adult that can make its own babies.
These pictures show the life cycle of a raccoon.

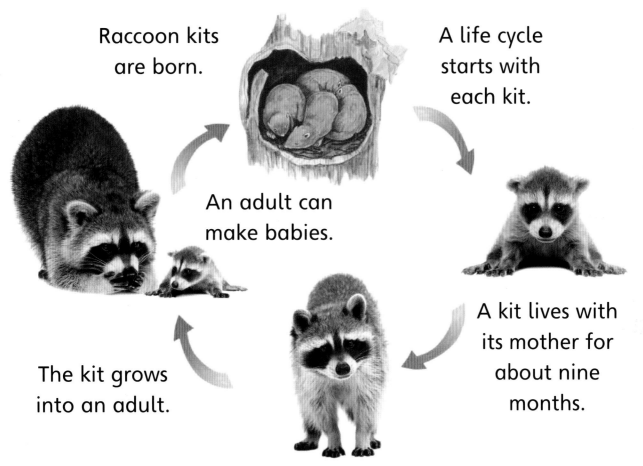

Raccoon kits
are born.

A life cycle
starts with
each kit.

An adult can
make babies.

A kit lives with
its mother for
about nine
months.

The kit grows
into an adult.

Learning as they grow

Baby animals must learn to do many
things before they become adults.
They need to learn how to
find food and stay safe.
The fox kits below are learning to hunt.

fox kits

Which baby animal is learning to fly?

Which one is learning to climb?

Which one is learning to run?

baby owl
(owlet)

baby
raccoon
(kit)

baby horse (foal)

13

Looking alike

Some baby animals look like their mothers, but they are much smaller. Do the animals on these two pages look like their mothers?

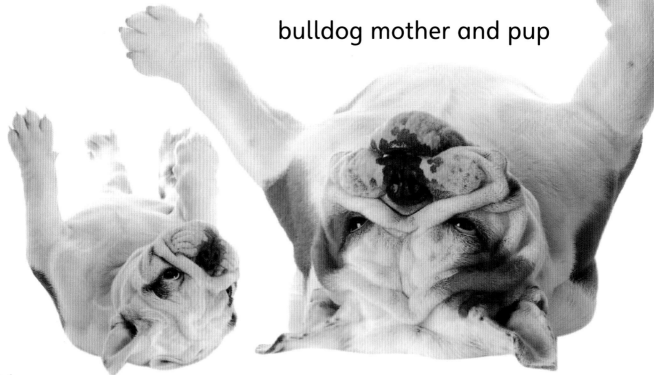

bulldog mother and pup

dolphin mother
and calf

lion mother
and cub

lynx mother
and cub

Changing their coats

Some baby animals do not look exactly like their mothers or fathers.
Their bodies change before they become adults.
Some animals **molt**, or shed, their skin, fur, or feathers.

old skin

new skin

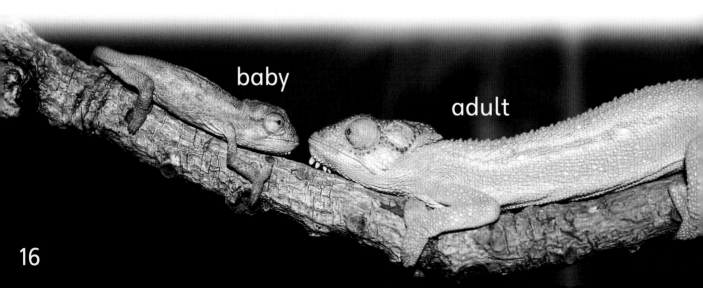

baby

adult

down

feathers

Barn owlets are covered with soft fuzzy **down**,
but they need feathers for flying.
The owlets molt their down and grow feathers.

Baby arctic foxes are born in summer with gray fur.
Before winter, their gray fur starts to molt.
By winter, new white fur has replaced the gray fur.

17

Butterfly changes

Some animals, such as butterflies,
go through big changes as they grow.
A butterfly starts life as an egg.
The egg hatches after a few days
and becomes a **caterpillar**.
The caterpillar eats and grows.

caterpillar

eggs

The caterpillar's skin
does not grow
with its body.
It gets too tight.
The caterpillar molts.

The caterpillar
molts four times.

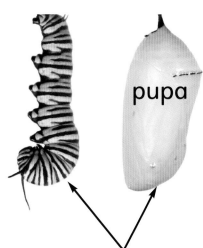

pupa

The caterpillar
hangs and becomes
a **pupa** or **chrysalis**.

It changes to a
butterfly inside
the chrysalis.
The butterfly
comes out.

The butterfly
dries its wings
and flies away.

Changes in newts

Newts are animals that start their lives in water and go through big changes by the time they become adults. These pictures show three big changes in a newt's body.

egg

egg

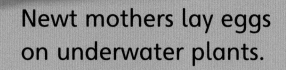
Newt mothers lay eggs on underwater plants.

Each egg hatches
into a **larva**.
In water, the larva
breathes with **gills**.
On land, an adult
newt breathes with
lungs, just as you do.

gills

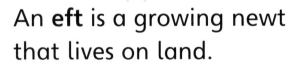

An **eft** is a growing newt
that lives on land.

An adult newt
is fully grown.

Did you know?
An animal's body going
through big changes is
called **metamorphosis**.
Newts, butterflies, and
dragonflies go through
metamorphosis.

Dragonfly changes

Some animals have only two big changes during metamorphosis. A dragonfly has only two big changes. After the dragonfly hatches, it is a **nymph**. The nymph grows and becomes an adult.

adult dragonfly

nymph

egg

22

Words to know and Index

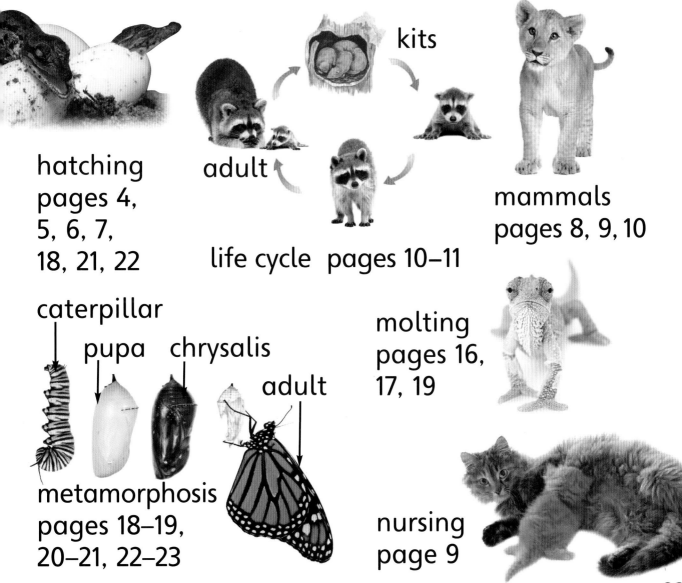

hatching
pages 4,
5, 6, 7,
18, 21, 22

kits

adult

life cycle   pages 10–11

mammals
pages 8, 9, 10

caterpillar

pupa   chrysalis

adult

molting
pages 16,
17, 19

metamorphosis
pages 18–19,
20–21, 22–23

nursing
page 9

Notes for adults

Objectives
- to teach children how animals change
- to teach children the similarities and differences in the way animals come to life (hatching, being born)
- to introduce life cycles
- to show children how animals change as they grow (physically and in abilities)
- to introduce metamorphosis

Before reading the book
Ask the children to guess what the cover animal might be and what kind of animal it is. (A newt is an amphibian like a frog.)
"How have your pets changed?"
"How do you change?"
Show pictures of a dog, bird, lizard, newt, dragonfly, and butterfly.
Ask them to guess which animals have the most changes in their bodies from the time they are babies to the time they are adults.

Questions after reading
"Which animals hatch?" (snakes, turtles, crocodiles, birds)
"How do mammal mothers feed their babies?" (They nurse them.)
"What do baby animals learn?"
(how to find food, stay safe, run quickly, climb trees, fly)

"Have you ever seen an animal change?"
(Ask the children to describe animal changes they have seen in books, on TV, or in their pets.)
"Name four ways that children grow and change."

Activities: Life-cycle centers
Set up five life-cycle centers, each containing an illustration of a life cycle of a different animal (dragonfly, newt, raccoon, sea turtle, butterfly). Have the children draw and label the life cycles.

Dig it!
Create actions for some of the stages of a sea turtle's life cycle (or that of another animal).
- eggs: all the children curl up on the carpet
- eggs hatch: children make a crackling sound and come up to their knees
- digging out: the children make digging actions as they pretend to dig themselves out of the sand
- crawl on the sand to the ocean and swim away

Extension
Introduce the **It's fun to learn about baby animals series** by Bobbie Kalman.
(Guided reading: J)
Children will have fun learning about the life cycles of many adorable baby animals. There are books on chipmunks, lemurs, polar bears, wolves, bunnies, elephants, foxes, giraffes, pigs, raccoons, horses, puppies, cats, apes, reptiles, birds, deer, and bears. *Tadpoles to frogs* and *Caterpillars to butterflies* are about metamorphosis.

For teacher's guide, go to www.crabtreebooks.com/teachersguides